DERBY CHINA
THROUGH THREE CENTURIES

MYRA CHALLAND

© 1991

ISBN 0 946404 37 2

Printed and Published by
J. H. HALL & SONS LIMITED
Siddals Road, Derby

Printers and Stationers since 1831
Telephone: Derby (0332) 45218
Fax: (0332) 296146

THE DERBYSHIRE HERITAGE SERIES

Illustration[1] *Kedleston Hall*   **The Historic Derbyshire Home of the Curzon Family**

Collectors throughout the world acknowledge the beauty of the porcelain that has been manufactured in Derby for almost three centuries. It owns a special place in the story of ceramics and the history of the city.

Nowadays, 'Derby', as the porcelain is generally known, is more easily obtainable than when it was first produced for the proprietors of elegant town houses or mansions set in rolling parklands.

The lovely 18th century houses, as in illustration [1] were the setting for an often leisured lifestyle. Entertainment on the grand scale called for vast quantities of refreshments served from silver, crystal and porcelain. There were opportunities to compare possessions of which the latest — and probably most envied — may have been porcelain.

Porcelain was that magical, white, translucent material for so long obtainable only from the Far East, brought either by intrepid travellers or later by clippers of the East India Company, carrying in their holds tea, silk, jade, lacquerware and porcelain from China, to eager customers in England.

Or perhaps an aristocratic family may have ordered at enormous expense, a finely painted tableware service or figure group, not from China, or even from those prestigious factories in Meissen, Sèvres or Chelsea, but from Mr Duesbury's fine factory in Derby.

The porcelain factory was founded on Nottingham Road, near ancient St Mary's Bridge, around 1748,[2] where a Huguenot jeweller, André Planche experimented with ingredients which he hoped would produce a similar material to that being successfully developed at Meissen, in Germany. To this talented man the first porcelain made in Derby can be attributed. He was joined, in 1756, by William Duesbury whose work had previously been that of porcelain decorator in London, and who now brought his considerable business

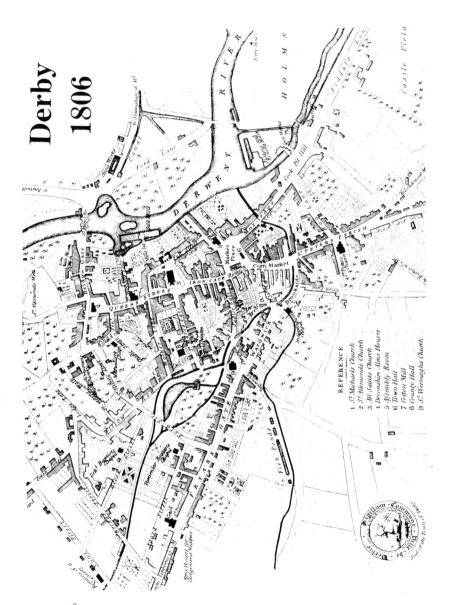

Derby 1806

REFERENCE

1 St Michaels Church
2 St Alkmonds Church
3 All Saints Church
4 Devonshire Alms Houses
5 Assembly Room
6 Town Hall
7 Cotton Mill
8 County Hall
9 St Werburgha Church

Illustration [2]

acumen to this new venture. The financial backing was contributed by a local banker, John Heath, who had earlier been active in a creamware business on Cockpit Hill in Derby. These three men, with their varied talents, joined with the factories of Bow, Chelsea, Bristol and Newcastle in following the lead given by the German, Italian and French companies in the making of European porcelain. Bristol and Newcastle survived barely two years, whilst Bow and Chelsea went bankrupt within 25 years and were taken over, with factories at Vauxhall and Kentish Town, by William Duesbury. Many other companies became involved in the manufacture of porcelain. Because of Duesbury's pioneering skill *Derby* pieces became style leaders, though still 1,000 years behind the Far East in expertise.

During that 1,000 years, Chinese porcelain had seeped, then flooded into Britain, exciting collectors of rare and beautiful objects by its delicate white translucency. However, those who had craved to possess Chinese porcelain now craved for the newer, more fashionable alternative, first produced under the banner of Saxony in Meissen in 1710. In spite of rigorous attempts to keep the method secret, first France and then England acquired the expertise to produce figurines and tableware. Meissen produced hard-paste porcelain similar to that made by the Chinese. It demanded a 'hard' or higher temperature firing than the softpaste English and French porcelain. The results were very similar in appearance except that the German body was bluer than the creamier coloured French and English soft paste was. However, much less suitable for utilitarian use, having a tendency to 'fly apart'.

Many of the early figures and patterns were taken from paintings, drawings and sculpture and inter-copied between factories. The earliest influence was from China, later from Japan, and in turn those countries copied the emerging European styles in order to sell their own versions to the West.

Copying styles was an international activity. The dwarves, illustration [3], a pair of German figures originally taken from a 17th century drawing, was copied both at Mennecy in France and at Chelsea. The Chelsea mould was acquired by William

Illustration [3]

Illustration [4]

Duesbury when the London company went bankrupt, and since 1769 the figures have been made at Derby.

The Meissen influence was lost when the factory was destroyed in the Prussian invasion of Saxony. An attempt by Prussia to re-establish the industry in Berlin failed, thus allowing the French to rise as the leading European stylists. The paintings of Boucher and Watteau, the sculpting talents of Falconet, wonderful colour and gilding were from 1756 England's major source of competition from Europe.

The early *Derby* figures which show the French style, in dress and in derivation, appear from about 1760 to 1790; a typical figurine of this period is shown in illustration [4]. Chelsea had also adopted similar ideas, and after the takeover of their factory by William Duesbury, both lines of production had common features. Bow, which had originally called its factory 'New Canton', and retained a chinoiserie style, failed similarly to Chelsea, mainly due to the problems of producing a wasteful, luxurious, expensive type of ware. This was in spite of catering for a slightly lower class of customer who still retained an interest in Chinese style blue and white or enamelled objects.

During the establishment of Duesbury's factory, which coincided with the failure of others, there were new porcelain ventures beginning. However, only *Derby* porcelain remains of that exciting stage of today's china industry.

Many early shapes were taken from Chinese and Japanese ware — the tea bowl (preceding today's handled cup), the teapot created from a wine pot shape, the octagonal and bowl shaped plates which appeared in their European form almost until the end of the 18th century. Patterns too were copied. The earliest styles included flowers, birds and fruit, with some figure and landscape subjects. The flower spray, adapted from Japanese porcelain of the 17th century, was used almost universally and survives today at many factories, on many differing bodies. It is the oldest *Derby* pattern, having been in use since the 1750s, and is known today as 'Derby Posies'.

Further patterns, shapes and moulds increased Derby's range when Chelsea and then Bow went bankrupt and were acquired by William Duesbury, along with the factories at

Vauxhall and Kentish Town. Experiments previously carried out on body and glaze at those factories also proved useful, and their adoption helped to improve and perfect production of *Derby* in the 1770s and 1780s. Chelsea's major contribution was to colour and glaze, whilst Bow had been experimenting with the addition of bone ash in order to give additional flexibility to the porcelain recipe.

The failure of the London factories was a symptom of the difference between England and the Continent. All other European porcelain was manufactured solely for the ruling houses. Profit was not a consideration. In England, a failed kiln firing or an expensive mistake in mixing and drying clay could tip a company over the edge into bankruptcy.

Derby's ability to survive may have been sheer good luck, or it may have been shrewd business management. Nevertheless the survival of the factory may well have had something to do with William Duesbury's careful supervision of potting and decoration, and his tireless travelling between the factory and the London showroom. He extracted from employees agreements to keep factory secrets, and instituted work study methods to make sure that men were paid only at the rate agreed for the completion of satisfactory work.

The china factory on Nottingham Road was built on a site bounded by today's Wood Street and Fox Street. Illustration [5] shows a view of the buildings sketched by a former Derby artist, Moses Webster, with an accompanying ground plan [6] of both William Duesbury's house and the adjoining factory buildings. This area has recently been the scene of some excitement, when old spoil heaps from a later addition to the earliest buildings were revealed during work on a new community centre. The presence of wasters has for years been apparent to the occupants of the surrounding houses, many of whom have dug up old *Derby* along with their potatoes and Brussels sprouts. Since these wasters were broken and useless to all but an historian, they must have proved an annoying side product of gardening.

Much of the very early *Derby* ware which exists today is figurine work, produced either as table decoration (a more durable version of the sugar or marzipan coloured and gilded

figures of the Mediaeval and Tudor period) or incorporating candleholders or sweetmeat baskets. The body (a clay mixture of any type suitable for shaping and firing in a kiln) in the early years was not very strong, tending to crack on contact with hot liquids. With experimentation it was sufficiently strengthened to offer competition to the oriental porcelain, which in spite of its long journey from China was still less expensive than its European counterpart.

Gradually, adaptions of early examples began to appear: handles on cups, strainers in spouts, condiment shelves on plates. The fashionable hostess was keen to serve exotic delicacies, bringing the ice pail into use to freeze and chill fruit, wine or sorbets. These were loosely based on the silver wine cooler or monteith, with a recessed lid and space beneath an inner liner for natural ice to produce the desired level of chilling.

The ice was skimmed from lake and stream in winter, kept in the icehouse or game larder in a cool area, and fetched as required throughout the warm months. Hopefully the supply would remain frozen until the frosts returned.

PLAN of Mr. Duesbury's Garden, House, and Manufactory, Derby.

COPIED FROM OLD DEED OF LEASE TO BLOOR IN 1815.

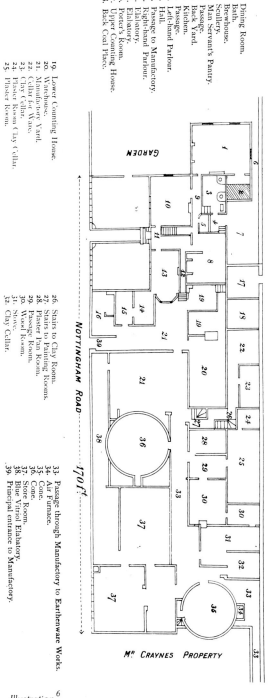

1. Dining Room.
2. Bath.
3. Brewhouse.
4. Scullery.
5. Man Servant's Pantry.
6. Passage.
7. Back Yard.
8. Kitchen.
9. Passage.
10. Left-hand Parlour.
11. Hall.
12. Passage to Manufactory.
13. Right-hand Parlour.
14. Elabatory.
15. Elabatory.
16. Porter's Room.
17. Upper Counting House.
18. Back Coal Place.

19. Lower Counting House.
20. Warehouse.
21. Manufactory Yard.
22. Cellar for Ware.
23. Clay Cellar.
24. Plaster Room Clay Cellar.
25. Plaster Room.

26. Stairs to Clay Room.
27. Stairs to Painting Rooms.
28. Plaster Pan Room.
29. Passage Room.
30. Wood Room.
31. Stove.
32. Clay Cellar.

33. Passage through Manufactory to Earthenware Works.
34. Air Furnace.
35. Cone.
36. Cone.
37. Store Room.
38. Blue Vitriol Elabatory.
39. Principal entrance to Manufactory.

Illustration 6

The beautiful classical houses, with their fashionable furniture and elegant decoration, were of course totally insanitary. The provision of pots in the sideboard cupboards to accommodate the gentlemen after their port, and perhaps a close-stool in the bedchamber, were the only provisions made for comfort. Some means of sweetening rooms had to be found. The answer was pot-pourri for which elaborate containers were produced,[7] both at Derby and elsewhere.

In a period when production of porcelain was difficult, expensive and painstaking, the majority of pieces produced were utilitarian, but decoratively exquisite, featuring flowers, exotic birds, insects and landscapes.

Armorials, with their overtones of breeding and aristocratic lineage, had long been used to emphasise power, position and prestige. They had previously featured on Chinese porcelain, commissioned by English families and painted by Chinese artists. The designs were sent to China with

Illustration [7]

11

descriptive notes, such as 'Red' 'Black' 'Green' in the appropriate places. Since few Chinese understood English the words were reproduced on the finished armorial. Figures appearing in the design sometimes arrived in European dress but with Chinese faces.

Having armorial decorations completed in England avoided such disconcerting mistakes. But even English workmen produced bizarre results, as when for instance, animals from other lands were required in designs.

Landscapes, real or imaginary, featured splendidly. Many reflected the customers' possessions, such as a magnificent service made for the Duke of Devonshire which was decorated with paintings of the Duke's many houses, or as on the Kedleston Vase illustrated on the cover, where the Hall is depicted in all its newly created glory, surrounded by its deer and deer park. The vase illustrated was originally one of a garniture of five, created to Adam's overall design for the Hall. Two more of these five we know to be in the museum at Indianapolis, but the remaining two seem to have vanished. Some reader may trace them in a far-flung corner of a foreign museum.

The Scarsdales of Kedleston have been valued customers of the Derby works for over 200 years. The portrait room at Kedleston Hall used to contain a fabulous display of c.1769 *Derby* porcelain but since acquisition of the Hall by the National Trust most of that fine collection is now in the family's private apartments, and not available to delight the visitor. A lovely botanical service from this period is, however, still on show in its original setting.

Botanical dishes were fashionably used to portray unusual and exotic plants introduced into England by explorers, and frequently grown in the wonderful glasshouses of the wealthy, following the opening of Kew Gardens to the public in 1774. This first resulted in the recording of specimens in great 'library' books which were intended to be left casually on view for guests to admire, much as 'coffee table' books are used today. Copies of these books were sent from London, to be used by the Derby artists when painting botanical dishes. The use of these decorative specimens on sets of dishes marked the owner of such porcelain services as erudite, travelled and possibly the possessor of the original plants.

From around 1771 a new fashion from France of using porcelain in a once-fired, unglazed state to imitate marble statuary was adopted. Continental factories produced this type of body, but at Derby it reached its finest form. Fine-grained, ivory in tone, satin-smooth, first produced at Sèvres reputedly to please Marie Antoinette, bisque became extremely popular but very expensive, since there was neither glaze nor decoration to mask small flaws. Less than perfect examples might have a strategic flower or leaf spray positioned over a discolouration or area of pitting, and were sold at a lower price. Subjects were usually classical, copies perhaps of full-sized statuary, or of Angelica Kauffmann subjects. Some of the most prized examples of Derby bisque occur in the clocks made by the Frenchman, Vuillamy, decorated and supported by classical figures. The figures for these clocks had to be made with holes in hands or feet so that they could be screwed into place.

The earliest mention of animal bone in *Derby* to provide strength, translucency and whiteness, appears in connection with bisque. No proportions are given, no recipe has been found. Later attempts to reproduce it were unsuccessful.

The satiny surface was originally achieved by accident, whilst firing bisque in a kiln alongside glazed ware. The vaporised glaze was deposited onto the bisque surface; later the same effect was accomplished by painting the saggar (a large fired-ware box used to protect objects being fired from coal fume discolouration) with glaze, so that it would vaporise in the same way.

Part of the high cost of bisque was its temperamental reaction to the 18th century kiln. This, as can be seen in illustration,[8] consisted of an oven (into which the saggars containing wares to be fired were stacked) and an outer bottle-shaped chimney.

After loading, the entrance was bricked up. Immense heat having already been reached before loading, the fuelling of the various firemouths around the base of the oven was carefully watched for 2 to 3 days during firing. Even in the coolest part of the kiln, bisque figurines sometimes melted or distorted very badly, leading ultimately to the need for a separate bisque kiln. This was never built, and bisque production was abandoned as unprofitable after the end of the century.

Illustration [8]

The bottle kilns were, with minor modifications, used from the end of the 17th century until the 1950s. They are now only to be seen where evidence of old methods is preserved, such as at the Gladstone Pottery Museum in Longton, Stoke-on-Trent. During the period when these kilns were universally in use for all types of potting they dominated the skylines and blackened the air for almost 200 years.

The early years at Nottingham Road, when the bottle kilns were in use, must have been extremely uncomfortable for the 200 or so employees, even though the factory was probably a good example of an industrial building of its time. Factories tended to follow the plan for farm buildings, with an owner's house surrounded by workshops. The ground plan for the Nottingham Road building is illustrated on page 10.

Though up to date by 18th century standards, the buildings with small, high windows would have been dark, cold in winter, hot in summer and surrounded by industrial hazards: toxic colours, dust disease, intense heat from kilns and drying stoves were some of the unpleasant problems workers encountered in their long working day.

'Wedging' clay, still done by craft potters, which involved cutting and slapping together sections of solid clay to mix it to a suitable consistency for shaping, ruined lungs and back. This work was often done by cheap labour — women and young boys. The lifting and loading of heavy saggars on a padded cap by climbing up and down the high ladders known as 'osses' inside baking hot ovens, burned away hair, eyebrows and moustaches. Mixing and dipping ware into glaze vats filled with lead crystal particles caused lead poisoning. Painting and gilding in poor light ruined eyesight; bending over for long periods caused distortion of the spine and neck.

The Fireman was probably one of the most valuable employees. It was his skill in supervising the fuelling and regulation of heat in the kiln which ensured a successful firing. He was required to be constantly alert over a period of 72 to 80 hours — testing, governing the feeding of firemouths, gradually heating and then cooling to completion. This was done for both the biscuit (first firing of clay to a hardened state) and for glost (the surface sealed with glass which had fused to the surface by heat). Unloading was carefully carried out, for both firings, with greater care accorded to the glazed pieces.

This was an immense responsibility. The large quantities of beer brought to the Fireman constantly, by a small boy whose task this was, kept his thirst under control. Checking the state of firing involved withdrawing pieces of porcelain at regular intervals. The method used for *Derby* was to scrutinise the piece removed through darkened glass to cut out the glare from the kiln. This was evidently sufficiently important to have the fireman sign a secrecy document, in which he contracted never to reveal the method to any other person. Spitting onto the withdrawn object to check its condition was apparently also part of the process.

Our knowledge of this part of *Derby's* early history is largely due to a cheerful, chatty book written in 1875 by John Haslem, a talented painter in enamels who worked at the Nottingham Road factory for many years. Much of the content of his book concerns the employees he knew and remembered more for their eccentricities than for their work, although he expresses great admiration for those whose work he knew well.

He describes the earliest factory buildings as 'replete with taste and utility', and tells us also of the additional buildings of 50 years later; there was a connecting passage between the two which was known as 'Birdcage Walk' because of its heavy wire covering. The buildings stood back from Nottingham Road behind existing homes and public houses. One of those, the 'Punch Bowl', was much used in the factory's hey-day.

The newer group of buildings was intended originally for the production of earthenware (a cheaper type of body, heavier and opaque). Though there was an engine house to provide power, no engine was ever used.

The earliest factory buildings were closed sometime between 1835 and 1845. Later, on the same site, a nunnery built for the Order of St. Joseph was designed by Pugin, the architect of St. Mary's church in Derby. Because the site was considered unhealthy for the nuns (though obviously had not been considered so for the workers) the nunnery was demolished in 1863. The later group of factory buildings survived until 1848, when the Nottingham Road site was abandoned.

THE CONVENT OF ST. JOSEPH, DERBY

The period which Haslem's book describes covers not only the lifetime of William Duesbury (1725-86), but also that of his son, William Duesbury II (1763-96). Both were astute business men and shrewd managers. The second William Duesbury had carried the company on in fine style between the date of his father's death and his own, ten years later. Many aristocratic and royal customers had been enticed to buy and the Royal Warrant was received from George III c.1775. The Crown was incorporated thereafter in the factory mark. The award of the right to use the crown in the name was in response to royal figure groups produced about this time. One of those depicted George III in Vandyke costume, with crown and sceptre on a cushion before him. Another showed Queen Charlotte, Princess Charlotte and Princess Sophia, whilst the third group comprised the Prince of Wales (later George IV), Prince Frederick William and Prince Edward playing with a dog. All these figures were in bisque, with blue and gold enamelling on the plinths. The modelling was apparently taken from one of Zoffany's monumental paintings of 1770. The figure groups were also monumental; possibly the King was so stunned by the attempt to reproduce so many of his offspring that he felt some reward was due.

Modelling of the kind which was most admired was by Pierre Stephan, Jean-Jacques Spaengler and William Coffee. All were talented and produced lively figures. The Elements,

17

still made today, were created by Stephan, a Swiss, who had trained at Wedgwood. He also specialised in generals and admirals (presumably whilst their names were popularly known), often in bodies other than porcelain, often in black or grey.

William Coffee was required to produce a shepherd figure, to pair with a shepherdess already modelled by Spaengler. This he did by using a model of Adonis, one of a series of antique casts given to the factory by Joseph Wright of Derby. To Wright's naked figure Coffee added clothing, a dog and a sheep. The finished figure [9] was pronounced to be finer than the Spaengler shepherdess. Coffee also modelled in plaster and terracotta. He is known to have modelled an enormous figure of Aesculapius, the father of medicine, for the roof of the Derbyshire Royal Infirmary. His first attempt blew up in the kiln, with a tremendous loss of money to the artist. The generous people of Derby subscribed towards a replacement.

Spaengler, whilst talented, was a difficult man, often in debt, often imprisoned, and often causing problems for his employer.

Illustration [9]

Haslem tells us quite a lot about a partner taken by William Duesbury II after the death of his father. Michael Kean was a very fine miniaturist and a forward-thinking business man, whose idea it was to extend the original factory buildings onto a plot of leased land adjacent to the original site. But on the debit side he was a wild-tempered Irishman, whose rages encouraged workmen to keep handily by them some form of weapon as protection against his physical attacks upon them. He was also an opportunist. He married his partner's widow most expeditiously and acquired both her share in the company and the Duesbury money, since in those days a married woman's money automatically became that of her husband. They later separated.

Kean was disliked by both family and workers, and was finally forced out of the business. He returned to Ireland, leaving the factory in 1811, without a satisfactory manager in charge.

William Duesbury III was a boy of ten years when his father died, and even when adult took no part in the running of the company. He later emigrated to America, where he remained until his death. The management of the factory devolved upon Robert Bloor, a clerk, who took over the lease of the site and the day-to-day running of the business. Robert Bloor was not a potter. He knew little about the technicalities of making or decorating porcelain and he had inherited many problems, principally financial. Bloor had offered to buy the business by instalments from Kean and the Duesbury family for £5,000. For this, and his creditors, Robert Bloor had to find enough money to satisfy their demands and to keep the company afloat.

The Bloor period of management coincided with the use of the new bone china body, introduced around the 1790s, and also the use of the newer, heavier oil colours for decoration. These two changes, along with the adoption of mercury gilding which replaced the honey gold of the 18th century, resulted in very richly coloured, elaborately gilded, flamboyant designs known as 'Japans'. These patterns were English copies of Japanese export pieces made purely to comply with Western taste, in cobalt blue, iron red and gold.

The Japanese called them 'Brocade' patterns and the first English examples seen around 1780-90 excited public interest immediately.

The English versions of these patterns were made by virtually every factory, in every type of ceramic body, in a profusion of variations. These patterns were called 'Imari' in Japan, since that was the only port from which porcelain left that country. The name also served to disguise the location of the many small sites of production from competitors. English Imaris were varied enormously by the use of the Japanese motifs arranged in numerous ways to produce new and exciting combinations.

The profuse pattern style served as an advantage for Bloor. The heavy, rich colours and gold appealed to the taste of the King, George IV, who continued to patronise the factory as he had done as Prince of Wales. There was another advantage, too. The dramatic bold colourings served to conceal, with decoration, the minor flaws which would previously have made finished pieces unacceptable to customers. This meant full utilisation of kiln loads, with the finished goods being sold in enormous auctions in order to bring in badly-needed money as quickly as possible. This method of selling had originally been used by William Duesbury, until the opening of the London showrooms allowed more subtle means of reaching the customer.

The desperate, demanding years brought about serious illness, and for the last twenty years of his life Bloor was in an asylum. During his illness the factory was under the control of John Haslem's uncle, James Thomason. From 1844 Robert Bloor's daughter and her husband, Thomas Clarke, were responsible, although business was steadily declining. They fought to avert the financial disaster which became inevitable in 1848, when Bloor died. The company which the Duesburys had created, which had succeeded in spite of rejecting the 'factory system' established by Josiah Wedgwood, and which had rivalled Europe's finest products for almost a hundred years, died too.

Cargoes of ware, moulds, patterns and machinery were ferried in twenty barges to the factory of Samuel Boyle, the major buyer, at Fenton in Stoke-on-Trent. Many of those whose employment had gone were faced with the need to find work elsewhere: for many the long walk to Stoke-on-Trent to other pot banks, for others the necessity of moving into other industries. With a fine work-force scattered, it is fortunate for us today that these artists, gilders, potters and modellers, many of them still connected to families in the Derby area, have been immortalised by John Haslem.

Haslem has recorded their names, for collectors of old porcelain, for historians, for family histories and for the company's archives. Their talent, their eccentricities, their failures and successes are all part of Derby history.

Of these people the best known names are probably those of the artists, since those who shaped and fired the clay seem to have been less well remembered, and of those artists perhaps the flower painters are seen as synonymous with *Derby*. Flower painting belonging to 18th century *Derby* was begun by Edward Withers in the early years, and continued by William Billingsley, William 'Quaker' Pegg and George Complin. All were an inspiration for those who followed. The flower theme continues today.

Sadly, Edward Withers died in distress and was buried by his workmates. His trouble does not seem to have been caused either by lack of talent or success but by poverty, an ever present spectre.

Landscape is important for many painters, and this type of decoration was carried out by Thomas 'Jockey' Hill; the Brewer brothers, Robert and John, George Robertson and Daniel Lucas. The early methods were based on watercolour painting, particularly in the style of Paul Sandby and J. M. W. Turner which was the fashionable trend at the time. Light, airy, delicate colours were used until superseded by the heavier oil colours of the 19th century. Each artist had an individualism, which is still a source of discussion among modern ceramics experts who are sometimes, but not inevitably correct, since there was much copying of both subjects and style. The Prentice Plate,[10] painted by William Billingsley, for instance, was kept in the painting shop for 70 years for use as a guide for apprentices in the art of painting flowers. Later John Haslem picked up this model plate in 1856 for 2/-d in a London shop.

Billingsley, in addition to being a very fine painter, was also the possessor of an unfortunate character. He was restless and ambitious, most anxious not only to decorate porcelain but to control the whole operation: to mix, shape and fire perfect porcelain. In order to do this he joined John Coke, a landowner, in 1796 to establish the *Pinxton* (Derbyshire) factory, where he took charge of the entire range of skills necessary to produce high quality, finely decorated porcelain.

Illustration [10]

This factory, as was the case with many others, failed to survive and Billingsley began a series of wanderings: to Mansfield, Torksey, Worcester, Nantgarw, Swansea and Coalport. He seems to have been an unhappy man, always desperately short of money. He apparently deserted his wife, possibly married bigamously and was constantly pursued by debt collectors. He is known to have changed his name at least once, if not more often, but whether to avoid wives or debtors we shall never know. In spite of the talent he displayed wherever he was employed, he was buried in a pauper's grave in Coalport. It is to be hoped he derived pleasure from his work, since little else in his life seems to have gone right for him.

'Quaker' Pegg, also a very fine flower painter, acquired his title from his religious views. He originally belonged to the Calvinists, later joined the Baptists and then the Friends. His views seem always to have been extreme. His adoption of the Quaker ideals was carried much further than by others who worshipped with him, particularly in his ultimate rejection of decorative work, which he felt went against the true teaching of God's law. This became the reason for his leaving the painting of porcelain.

From 1796 to 1801 he had worked at Nottingham Road, producing wonderfully detailed reproductions of the flowers he knew from his father's garden. Many of these were recorded in sketch books, but these records he finally burned. Only one of the books remains, painted when he returned to the factory after a disastrous period during which he worked in the Nottingham hosiery industry. He was similarly unhappy with this type of work, since he was expected to produce stockings decorated with 'clocks', which were decorative patterns running up from the ankle shaping of the stockings.

Pegg's return to the porcelain industry was short-lived. He again left and opened a huckster's shop, near to the factory and his friends, on Nottingham Road, The shop was close to a small canal bridge known for years as 'Pegg's Bridge'. Pegg's devoted wife, Ann, must have been relieved when her husband found a way to solvency which neither distressed him, nor which he felt to be wrong in the sight of God.

'Jockey' Hill was well-remembered by Haslem and his contemporaries more for his well-trained pony than for his undoubted painting talent. The animal carried Hill to work each day, then returned to its stable alone. In the evening the pony would again be found waiting for his master to take him back home. Hill painted fine landscapes of local interest, using only the stumps of three lost fingers to hold his brush.

Haslem took a great delight in recording that William Watson never talked to any of his fellow employees, although he occasionally shouted 'Georgie' for no apparent reason whilst working. He also spent his meal periods in the willow trees bordering the factory yard. He never seemed to eat.

Many of the workmen, when dissatisfied, would take their

skills elsewhere. William Dexter was one whose travels took him to the Australian goldfields, an enormous and dangerous journey. He was evidently an original. His eccentricities revealed themselves through his adoption of Hungarian dress and the smoking of a hookah. He encouraged his wife to wear that most practical but unacceptable costume, bloomers. Amelia Bloomer would have been most gratified, but the couple must have been regarded as outlandish.

Someone far more conformist was John Whitaker, a modeller best known for his 'peacock among flowers', a figure still made today [11]. Haslem tells us of a visit made to the factory by Mr Sam Fox, of Osmaston Hall. This gentleman brought to Mr William Locker the Managing Clerk a piece of 'continental bisque' which he thought might act as a model of excellence for the Derby artists and modellers. Locker, a man of few words, called John Whitaker to see this figure, asking him who he thought might have made it. Back came the answer which Locker knew to be true. 'I made it, of course,' said Whitaker.

Illustration [11]

Derby bisque was often described as 'Continental' when offered for sale in London, since that carried more of a cachet.

Many of the Derby artists were skilled in other media, and either painted portraits or taught these skills to others. Some, like William Corden, were commissioned by aristocratic or royal sitters. Corden's commission was to paint a series of life-size portraits of Prince Albert's ancestors, whilst Haslem painted several royal portraits on ceramics which were exhibited at the 1851 Exhibition at Crystal Palace. Two of these, Queen Victoria and Prince Albert, painted in 1840, are now on show in the Royal Crown Derby Museum. Daniel Lucas also had a lucrative sideline as a specialist painter of inn signs in Derby.

There were, of course, other occupations for the very limited leisure time of workers in those days. Mundy Simpson, a gilder and Japan painter, was a very keen swimmer and also enjoyed playing football, especially Shrovetide football. This is a ball game peculiar to Derbyshire and today only played at Shrovetide in Ashbourne but earlier was also played in Derby town streets. It involves two teams, one playing 'uppards' and the other playing 'downards', and sees no avoidable obstacles. Simpson regularly jumped into the River Derwent with the ball, swimming to escape the opposing players.

Fishing was immensely popular with many of the employees. Tommy Tatlow not only caught fish, but also painted them. Perhaps the proximity to river and canal encouraged this simple occupation, or perhaps they found quiet riverside meditation soothing after long hours inside factory walls.

Tom Hancock, one of a family associated with both Nottingham Road and the later King Street factory, was, like Tommy Tatlow, a very keen fisherman, but his leisure time must have been limited, since he walked home to Nottingham on Saturday evening after work, and returned to Derby in time to begin work on Monday morning. He was apparently the first artist to mix and experiment with enamel colours, and also perfected a recipe (spelt 'receipt' in those days) for the toxic mercury amalgam gold which replaced honey gold (gold mixed with honey to a paintable fluid) at the beginning of the

19th century. This used six parts of gold to five parts of mercury.

George Robertson painted views of the interior and exterior of the Nottingham Road factory which we would dearly love to see today. They originally hung in the London showroom but were removed to a cellar, where they eventually fell apart from damp. His work for the factory was mainly of marine and landscape subjects, which are keenly collected.

Corden is known to have painted a mural of Darley Grove on a summer house wall overlooking the bowling green which at that time adjoined the 'Seven Stars' public house, kept by Tommy Tatlow. This must have been a wonderful antithesis, both to his miniature work on ceramics and his portraits of Prince Albert's relatives, with their gloomy Germanic expressions.

James Rouse, Senior, who worked at all three Derby factories and lived to a great age, worked with 'Quaker' Pegg, George Robertson, William Cotton (a landscape painter) and William Corden. He is recorded as saying that Pegg was very kind to the young apprentice painters. The group of friends, and the boys, gathered at night at Pegg's house, where he gave the youngsters lessons in painting and drawing. The only rewards he asked were the drawings the boys produced under his tuition. Rouse must have known many apprentices during his long employment as a painter of exquisite miniature flower groups and, more rarely, animal subjects. He must have had a wealth of experience to pass on to the young men.

The apprentices were trained over a seven-year period. Wages were four shillings per week until they were 18 years old, four shillings and six pence per week for the next two years and six shillings in the last year. Their 'stint', a determined amount of money deducted from their wages, was a premium which paid for their training.

The factory-trained apprentices augmented those skilled artists and modellers who brought their talent from other areas of artistic work, from other countries or factories. These valuable employees were paid highly for their work by the standards of the day. They were, however, quite often temperamental beings, difficult to control and often unwilling to work regularly or for the required normal 10½ hour day, six days a week. The factory system, even the relatively modified version in operation at Derby, was too new for workers readily to accept its restrictions on their liberty. It is difficult to realise that the idea of a structured working week became the norm only as a result of the progressive factory system, and the Victorian work ethic.

In order to keep his workers' noses to the grindstone, . William Duesbury using binding contracts 'sworn on the Bible and before God', and a system of fines (even for being in a part of the factory not their own place of work). He advanced loans to employees and also if necessary payment of their debts which he used like the wages he withheld sometimes for several weeks, to induce workers to complete outstanding work for him.

The modeller Jean-Jacques Spaengler, although very talented, was an unsatisfactory worker. He was loaned £30 by William Duesbury to pay off debts incurred in Derby, but once he had the money he set off to return to Switzerland. He was caught at Ramsgate and imprisoned. Friends stood bail for him, but once again he disappeared.

The painter James Banford was similarly unsatisfactory. He was deeply in debt to Duesbury, first for his fare to Derby and then also for the money required to bring his family to the town. He was a heavy drinker, unstable and a poor provider for his family, though deeply penitent when sober. To offset her husband's improvidence, Bernice Banford asked William Duesbury to supply her with painting work to do at home. She had previously similarly worked for Josiah Wedgwood.

This incident sparked off a minor revolt amongst the decorating staff against the employment of women, whom, they said, 'were responsible for spoiling the work'. A petition was signed and presented to William Duesbury to this effect, and it was many years before women were allowed to take part in the fine decoration of porcelain. They were, however, in later years employed in large numbers to do this work.

A short strike occurred in 1825-26 over the management decision to reduce the already hated piece work rates by one quarter, to combat the results of the depression in trade at that time. The reduction was eventually accepted by the men, although one worker indignantly said that 'Master should have been content to reduce it by one-third', causing much amusement to his fellow workers!

Even in those days work study was carried out. Both Edward Withers and William Billingsley were asked to time themselves when painting individual flowers and flower groups, in order that the work could be economically costed. 'Spies' were employed by the Duesburys to keep watch on workers' methods, and 'spies' to spy on the 'spies'. Recently in a standard textbook on work study written in the 1960s reference was made to a contract given to Thomas Mason, in 1792, to carry out a comparative study of workers' times, 'secretly'.

Several workers are recorded as having been dissatisfied with wages and conditions. Some moved to other potteries, sometimes long distances from Derby. Some, like 'Quaker' Pegg, returned. Others, like William Billingsley, continued to move on in search of either higher pay or greater recognition of their talent. John Mountford, who worked at Derby for many years, moved to the Copeland factory, where he attempted to reproduce the beautiful *Derby* porcelain bisque. Mountford failed to discover the exact proportions of the Bisque ingredients, but instead invented Parian. Parianware mimics marble most successfully; it is light in weight, easy to fire although time-consuming to produce. As is often the case with industrial discoveries he almost lost the credit for this invention. Alderman Copeland claimed publicly that he was the inventor, and it was only after much argument that Mountford received due recognition.

Many examples of the work of these talented artists and modellers were produced for local houses, not only Chatsworth, Kedleston or Belvoir but for less exalted homes. Henry Evans, of Allestree Hall, bought a complete service of 216 Botanical dishes, with wonderful exotic blooms painted on the famous *Derby* yellow ground.

In 1831 William Corden painted a service for William IV; it was so expensive it doubtless contributed to the final ruin of the company. There were 144 plates and 56 large pieces. The service cost £5,000. How long did the company have to wait to be paid? A comment about the payment of royal bills in William Bemrose's book, 'Derby, Bow and Chelsea porcelain' is very pertinent. When custom was lost from some royal circles, Lygo, Duesbury's agent in London, wrote to his employer that although they were completing work for the Duke of York, the Duke of Clarence was the only royal customer who paid his bills. However, royal patronage bestowed prestige, with profit coming from less exalted customers who regularly paid for manufactured goods.

Elaborate work on a dessert service for Belvoir Castle was done by George Robertson, who specialised in painting shipping. In 1820 the Persian Ambassador ordered 365 bowls and dozens of plates, solidly gilded inside and out, with chased figures and an inscription in Persian.

In 1830 a 250 piece service for the Earl of Shrewsbury was made, and decorated in underglaze green with a central crest and coronet. The ice pails to this service were shaped like the Warwick Vase. Imperfect pieces, which would not have been acceptable to the Earl, were used for other customers, with a piece of fruit in place of the central crest. Some of these pieces were bought by a Mrs Horsley of Pye Bridge. In 1871, 24 plates, 12 comports, a centrepiece and two sugar tureens cost £40.

In 1844 Queen Victoria ordered some extremely elaborate mounted plates. These were arranged in three tiers, with flower holders on the top. This was perhaps Victorian ostentation, where elaboration for its own sake began to replace the simpler elegance of the 18th century.

As not all houses were sumptuous, not all customers were wealthy, titled or royal. Of the patterns used, the Chantilly sprig was the one most likely to be seen in daily use in neighbourhood houses. This was a dainty pattern of small carnations or pinks, taken as the name implies from the French Chantilly factory's range. A similar much used pattern was the Angoulême sprig, originally used at the factory sponsored by the Duc d'Angoulême.

There were innumerable patterns using flowers of this kind, but by the 1800s the fashionable, exciting Japan patterns were being made by almost all English factories, on all kinds of ceramic bodies. Their rich red, blue and gold made them ideal under flickering candlelight. Many variations were produced, using the traditional Japanese stylised motifs. Examples of these early Japans are rare and expensive collectables.

The work of producing Japan patterns was traditionally for the underglaze cobalt blue (colour painted on to the biscuit surface before glaze is applied) to be done by women, once their work on decoration was accepted by the male staff. The more detailed red and gold (fired onto the surface of the glaze) was still done by men.

The cost of decoration depended on the number of firings needed. A simple wash was normally fired first, with more detailed, deeper colour being added in a second firing, making the piece a more expensive object.

Production costs were high, with labour costs outweighing all others. Though there is only sparse evidence available, it would seem that in this period the workers were paid reasonably well. Some costs were paid by the London end of the business, such as the purchase of gold, and the salary paid to the London agent, Lygo. A shop in Bath had been opened, following the example of Josiah Wedgwood, since Bath, next to London, was the haunt of the fashionable. This shop too was probably funded locally, and was managed by William Duesbury's brother-in-law, Richard Egan.

Overseas markets were limited. Irish dealers were unwelcome ('they fight low') and some ware went to Amsterdam, but the high import duties to protect Dresden and Sèvres from foreign competition made export unprofitable. Of course, these high duties helped English porcelain prices, while the French Revolution of 1789 prevented Sèvres exporting their wares to Britain.

The war with France led to the production of the *Derby* Rodney jug. This modelled Admiral Rodney's face for the spout and featured a cocked hat, with flowers painted on either side of the jug by George Withers. This object became part of a ritual meeting of local china workers and jewellers at the 'Fox and Owl' public house in Bridgegate, and was used for about 80 years for the purpose of serving ale to members of the group at each meeting. The jug later went to the 'Rose and Crown' in the Cornmarket, then to the 'Royal Oak', Market Place, and finally to the 'Crown and Thistle' in Chapel Street. The jug, which held five pints, was sold for £2 to Mr Ratcliffe, of Walton Hall, near Burton-on-Trent, when the club disbanded.

The period from around 1825 was increasingly difficult, when Robert Bloor's illness (Haslem suggests lunacy, some alcoholism, others worry and financial pressure), forced him to hand over control of the company to his daughter and son-in-law, and the managing clerk, William Locker. The political climate of revolution in Europe, and unrest in England as an aftermath of the 1832 Reform Act accentuated by the continued activities of the Chartists, were circumstances which, with the Irish Famine and the repeal of the Corn Laws, spelled disaster for an ailing company.

For those whose livelihood was thus to be cut off (many probably unaware that such a state of affairs was pending), the need to find new jobs meant a move to another town, another pot bank. For most that was Stoke-on-Trent, or even further afield. Incredibly, one or two, following the example of emigrating Irishmen, made America or Canada their goal.

Locker, for many years in charge of the day-to-day running of the company, was not one to run elsewhere if there was a chance of saving something from disaster. With a small group of skilled men and a boy, he found a new home for the business. The group moved moulds, machinery, raw materials and pattern books not already disposed of to other manufacturers to begin a new chapter in an old book.

The buildings chosen for the new venture were clustered on King Street, close to the 17th century 'Seven Stars' public house. This ancient site had accommodated a Roman-Christian St. Helen's church and Norman abbey, long gone. In its place had been built an imposing town house for the Fitzherberts, which was later occupied by Joseph Wright of Derby. The house was demolished to make way for a spar works which preceded the china factory. All evidence of industrial history is gone today but the main building fronting King Street is still there, opposite Pickford's St. Helen's

House. A drawing from an old photograph [12] taken at the turn of the century shows how comparatively unchanged is the facade today. The ground floor is now a shop whilst the upper floor has been adapted for flats.

After forty years connected with the old company, and furious at its closure, William Locker created a new organisation with Hill, Fearn, Sharp, Henson and Sampson Hancock. Like Locker, the Hancocks had been closely associated with the Duesburys almost from the beginning. This pioneering group was later joined by other ex-workers from the old factory. The early name of the King Street business was 'Locker & Co. late Bloor''. By 1859, this had changed to 'Stevenson, Sharp & Co.'. Stevenson was first a partner of Sharp and later of Sampson Hancock.

The company then adopted the old factory mark a crown over a 'D', with crossed swords, with the addition of the letters 'S' and 'H' when the partnership of Stevenson and Hancock began in 1863.

The details of factory marks are mainly of interest to collectors of old porcelain, but a surprising number of people find that they have in their homes pieces of *Derby* porcelain which bear these old marks, and therefore are more

Illustration [12]

32

interesting. A comprehensive list of marks appears in the Appendix.

The factory mark thus revived continued to be used until the merger in 1935 with the Osmaston Road factory. The role of the Osmaston Road factory has yet to be mentioned, but it played its part from 1877.

The style of workmanship at King Street was a continuation of the striving for quality which had been the aim of the Duesburys. Advertising at the time of the King Street factory's hey-day was 'everything is done by hand, by our craftsmen', and this in many ways coincided with the growing opposition to the increasing use of machines for ornamentation. The fiercest critic was William Morris who with the Arts and Crafts movement deplored the waste of skills and sought to re-create the ideals of the craftsman by their furniture, tapestries, fabrics, pottery, tiles and stained glass.

The King Street potters totally agreed with Morris' ideals, although his vision of making wonderful craft objects available to everyone was never achieved, since the high cost of labour and materials meant that only the wealthy could afford to buy.

The King Street premises continued production in craftsman's style, using methods and materials varying little from those used in earlier periods. They continued to make the old figures: Dwarfs, Elements, Seasons, Peacocks, Japans. The enamels used became brighter and for the first time faces were painted with blue eyes. Previously, on products from the Nottingham Road works only brown eyes had featured on the faces of the figures.

There was re-issue of previously successful figures made at the Nottingham Road factory, and also use of a brighter gold. This may well have been a less expensive gold than earlier, although possibly harder wearing.

The King Street factory never at any time employed more than 40 hands, compared to the reported numbers of 100 to 200 at Nottingham Road, so output would necessarily have been limited. It is known that china blanks (undecorated white) from other factories were brought in for decoration. This was, of course, done by many factories — William Duesbury is known to have bought in Chinese blue and white for embellishment and *Derby* blanks were used at both the Caughley factory and Chamberlain's of Worcester.

The painting both on figures and tableware was very beautiful. Colours from the past continued to be used; cobalt blue and iron red, of course, for Japans, and also the yellows and greens from the 18th century. Blues painted onto the surface of the glaze were used, in addition to the cobalt fired into the glaze.

Many Nottingham Road blanks, removed in 1848 to King Street, were later decorated there, giving continuity to production, but new ideas were developed. Large quantities of variously-shaped mirrors, with modelled-flower frames in glazed white, were made. The flowers, as today, were shaped from tiny scraps of clay which in the hands of skilled men like James Barnet, became sepals, petals, stamens, leaves and stems. Barnet's exquisitely modelled baskets of flowers were typical of this type of painstaking work. Flowers were also used to decorate figures as had been done since 1748, although the earlier flowers were relatively simple in shape. They were often called 'pastry-cutter flowers' since they were usually standard shapes throughout. Beautifully and naturally coloured, they bloomed everywhere, but especially on Whitaker's peacock.

The period after 1851 brought pressure to bear on all factories to improve design. The Great Exhibition had revealed what Morris so deplored. The machine-made, machine-decorated, sentimental, useless, over-ornamented horrors were crowded into every corner of the Crystal Palace. Instead of highlighting British superiority to the world, as Prince Albert had intended, the exhibits merely stressed the total lack of taste and refinement in Britain at that time.

Design in the 18th century arose from simple, uncomplicated forms decorated lightly in classical style. Since ornamentation could now be accomplished not by time, taste and skill but by pulling a lever, it appeared everywhere in chaotic profusion.

The ideas were a hotch-potch springing from the eclectic inspiration of the emerging middle classes. Rococo, Gothic and Renaissance were the most powerful influences, with

Gothic carrying moral and religious overtones.

Since the tiny King Street factory lacked mechanisation, these influences did not have great impact there. The factory continued to produce as it always had done. Sampson Hancock, a fine painter and manager, continued to run the company until 1866, when ownership went into the hands of James Robinson. He in turn was replaced by Larcombe and Paget, and finally until 1935 by Howard Paget alone.

By that time the earlier Japans, figures and tableware patterns from the past had been augmented by beautiful woven baskets similar to those made at Beleek in Ireland, animals (particularly dogs), commemoratives, candle snuffers, miniatures and figures of local oddities such as 'Belper Joe'. All of these are extremely collectable today.

Because of the rarity of King Street and early Nottingham Road Japans, and the interest shown by collectors, the recently produced reproduction set of six of these patterns is a credit to today's artists. They evoke the past beautifully, and their creation illustrates most effectively the contrast between the Imaris from this period and those which emerged, when interest in Imaris was renewed, in the closing years of the 19th century.

Throughout the period from 1877 the King Street factory had keen competition from a larger, more modern, newly established company formed by a Liverpool glass and china stockist and a Worcester potter. Having been denied a site in Worcester, doubtless to avoid becoming competitors for the Royal Worcester factory, these two gentlemen had taken over the site of the old Derby workhouse, built in 1830 to house the poor of the town. The site was enhanced by the Derby Arboretum, given to the town in 1840 by Joseph Strutt as 'a recreational area for the leisure of the labouring classes', and was in every way a 'garden' environment. This was to be Derby's 'garden factory' following the example of Bournville in Birmingham.

Edward Phillips and William Litherland's factory housed the newly formed Derby Crown Porcelain Company. The buildings in illustration [13] were completed in 1877, with all the finest and most modern equipment. No expense was spared

Illustration [13]   *Circa 1877*

Illustration [13]   *Circa 1950*

to make this the most modern factory in Europe. There were three biscuit (first firing) kilns and three glost (second firing) kilns. Over 400 hands were employed and fine new cottages were built to accommodate key workers close to the factory. Some of these, known as Ladygrove Cottages, still exist and many still house pottery workers today.

The new company set out to produce all the most fashionable and saleable wares. They were confident that no competition could be offered by the King Street company, in spite of its long pedigree and Royal Charter. The period offered manufacturers a very wide choice of products, colour and decoration with which to tempt the buyer, since science had advanced at a tremendous speed during the 19th century. Bone china was the main area of production, augmented by earthenware, Parianware and eggshell china.

Parian, the brainchild of John Mountford, had been adopted by most ceramic factories for its fashionable 'marble statuette' image. Earthenware was used for about twenty years and then abandoned. Eggshell, with its wafer-thin delicacy, was just the thing to grace the Victorian display cabinets in overstuffed drawing rooms.

The archaeologists who were returning to England with their spoils (sometimes illegally removed from ancient lands) brought to the South Kensington and British Museums Greek, Roman, Etruscan, Persian and Rhodian *objets d'art* which filled the acquisitive Victorian breast with envy. The desire to acquire articles like these paved the way for a wide range of decorative styles. Wonderful painting by talented artists created superb tableware and the uniquely useless decorative objects of the time, whilst the raised gold work inspired by Indian craftsmen was incredibly beautiful. The gold was layered, each layer being fired before each fresh application.

The Indian influence in design was inevitable following the manoeuvre by Disraeli to bestow on Queen Victoria the title of Empress of India. As the 'Jewel of the Empire', India gave to England many new words, colours, shapes, fabrics and designs, which gave new life to English design and manu-facture.

Another and even more important design element had

arisen in the 1870s, again influenced by events outside England. In 1868 Japan's dominant ruling house, the Shoguns, was overthrown, leading to rapid westernisation of its people. After her long enforced isolation from western civilisations, Japan began to export its artefacts across the world: woodcuts, fans, kimonos, ivory, lacquerware and of course porcelain. In the period since the early 18th century, when Chinese blue and white porcelain had lost its popularity in favour of European styling, Japan had taken and adapted Chinese images to fit Japanese ideology. For a whole new generation, blue and white porcelain and indeed all things oriental, were new and exotic.

The new enthusiasm was fostered by artistic groups, gasping with relief over something simple, tasteful and unusual. The 'Aesthetic Movement' gave it all the support of their society. Many painters, notably Whistler, included delicate pastel oriental elements in their paintings. This appealing simplicity led to a great demand for blue and white patterns to be made on all ceramic bodies. Staffordshire printed earthenware and stonewares, in addition to the more expensive bone china versions proliferated. During this period many lovely blue and white *Derby* patterns, both oriental, delft and geometric, were produced. Today, only 'Blue Mikado' remains in production from that time. The pattern follows Gilbert and Sullivan's interpretation of the Japanese theme.

A further response by the Derby factories, both Osmaston Road and King Street, as with those other potteries which produced Imaris, was to introduce new patterns in this particular idiom to satisfy customer demand.

The Japanese theme was directly responsible for the Art Nouveau movement of the 1885 to 1910 period, when swirling plant forms were used in all kinds of decorative work. This fairly short-lived style was always more popular in Europe than in England. It was gradually ousted by the powerful Art Deco movement which preceded the Modernism of the 1930s to 1950s. These later creative changes were never particularly strong at Derby, although the geometrics, both in pattern style and shape, appear in the pattern books during the 1930s and early 1940s. The traditional classic shapes, flower, bird and landscape themes, flat and raised gilding and, of course, the Japans remained the solid backbone of the *Derby* style.

The years from 1848, when King Street was established, and 1877, when the Osmaston Road factory came into being had seen enormous advances in technology within the ceramics industry. Most of these new ideas were either unacceptable or impractical at the King Street building, but became automatically incorporated in the new style productions at the Osmaston Road works. From the 1850s metal oxides had been used to produce not only a wide range of ceramic colours, but also to create lustres. Transfer printing was also more widely adopted. Overglaze printing, either from stone or wood blocks, had been used on ceramics, though rarely on early *Derby*, since the 1740s; these were expanded first to use underglaze printing in a single colour, later as a multi-colour operation. The use of copper plate engraving to re-create, on tissue paper, the artist's design was very time-consuming. The artist might spend several days producing a very finely detailed pencil or ink drawing of a complex design. To transfer this drawing to a copper plate might take an engraver up to six weeks of concentrated work. Originally each colour needed a separate plate, which would be over-printed. Eventually this could be done from a single engraved plate. Later it was also possible to produce gold and platinum transfers.

Solid colour, called ground laying, was added by coating the area to be coloured with several layers of thin oil dabbed on very carefully and smoothly, before coating the oiled surface with powdered colour from a cotton wool pad to give a completely even finish. The area not to be coloured had previously been covered with sugar water, which then washed off before the object was fired to fuse the grains of colour to a smooth gloss. For an expensive piece of ware this might be done two or three times to achieve a glorious depth of colour, impossible by earlier methods.

The adoption of different methods of preparing the clay for shaping removed many of the difficult practices of earlier years. One of the most important pieces of machinery was the filter press, which removed surplus water from slip (clay mixed with water to a liquid consistency), to produce the malleable material from which plates and dishes were made. The mechanical blunger which replaced hand-paddling of slip to prevent solid particles of clay from settling and impacting in the vats was also of enormous value economically. The general introduction within the industry of jolleys and jiggers, machines for shaping clay into or onto both flat and hollow plaster of paris moulds, was unpopular with workers. These, like most new methods, required fewer people. Instead of an earlier three-man team of baller-up (of clay), potter and runner (the boy who ran with shaped clay to the drying room), one man now could slice the clay, shape and then place it in the new revolving drying cabinets. Disastrous for workers — economical for manufacturers.

Another change made at this time was the use of liquid lead to replace raw powdered lead. Whilst still dangerous it was a move in the right direction, which eventually resulted in the use of fritted (heated) lead, where dangerous elements were burned out before its use in glazes. A truly exceptional glaze cannot be made without the inclusion of lead, although leadless glazes are used on products by some companies today.

Trade at this time was complicated by the collapse of the absolutist monarchies. The 1848 unrest surging through Europe on the heels of the French 1789 and 1830 revolutions had resulted in the establishment of republics. Factories such as Meissen, Vienna, Sèvres, whose products had been solely for the Crown, were now without patronage, and suffering the same struggle for survival as those in England. They were, of course, competing for the same markets.

This was also the time when Britain's code of Free Trade was badly damaged by American protectionism. Since English factories made to order , not for stock as American companies did, it was difficult for British factories to gauge demand.

In 1891 America introduced the McKinley Tariff, which required all companies to mark wares of all kinds with the country of origin. Manufacturers were supposed to include the word 'England' with their own mark. This is a useful addition for collectors, since it effectively helps to date otherwise obscure manufactured objects. It was, however, never adopted by the King Street company — rebellious as always. When the Copyright Act of 1911 was passed, America was not involved.

The use of marks on ceramics is a minefield for collectors, although *Derby* marks are well-documented. The early years include quite long stretches between mark changes, but the Osmaston Road company used year cyphers from 1880; impressed marks 1878 to 1900 and 'England' from 1891, 'Made in England' from 1902, 'Bone China' in the 20th century.

The King Street factory marks have already been mentioned, and their continuation of the old Nottingham Road mark commemorated their 18th century Royal Charter. The Osmaston Road company acquired their own Royal Charter in 1890, when the 'Royal' insignia was bestowed by Queen Victoria. This was as a result of a gift from 'The Loyal Ladies of Derby' for the Queen's Golden Jubilee in 1887.

Although Victorian belief in the sanctity of science and the inevitability of progress continued into the Edwardian period, the years which followed were to bring sensational changes. Traditions would be challenged, class barriers broken down, and radical changes would occur in the artistic field. The world of leisure, the pursuit of pleasure, which meant for many the acquisition of the trappings of wealth, were by the end of the reign of Edward VII gradually disappearing.

During the Edwardian period, however, those ornamental and often purposeless display objects which proclaimed money and status were still being produced, although Edwardian style was less oppressive. Elaborately painted and gilded, exotically shaped and very expensive, the wares at this time were produced by fine artists. Possibly the finest ceramic artist during this era was Desiré Leroy,[14] who worked at Osmaston Road.

Trained at Sèvres, he brought his French design flair first to the Minton factory in Stoke-on-Trent, and then to Derby. He introduced new methods, ideas and colours. His work shines out like a beacon. He was tremendously gifted in that he was

Illustration [14] circa 1900

totally adept at all types of decorative work: ground colour laying, painting and gilding. He particularly excelled at the use of delicately painted white or slightly tinted enamel on coloured grounds. He also painted exquisite flower panels, cupids, trophies, fruit and musical instruments with equal skill.

Of those who worked with Leroy, or were employed in decoration during that time, each had his unique style.

Landgraf painted in the archaic style beloved of Victorians, whilst Count Holzendorf painted delicious cherubs, John Joseph Brownsword favoured lovely children and James Rouse, Senior, mainly flowers but also portraits and animals. Rouse is interesting in that he worked at all three of the Derby factories, the only artist known to have done so. Whilst these important artists were relatively well-paid, the humbler decorating staff earned little.

The use of paste gilding replaced the earlier layered gold, achieved by painting on a china paste decoration, which was then fired in relief on the body of the plate or vase. The relief design was then heavily overlaid with gold.

This superbly painted and gilded ware was obviously never intended for use in the serving or the consumption of food; such a mundane purpose could never have been envisaged for these expensive works of art. Their obvious settings were a royal yacht or noble residence, Boule cabinet or Godwin sideboard.

A new factory wing at Osmaston Road was added in 1891 for copper plate engraving work which was intended for adding further decoration, with the main part of the ground laying, painting and gilding still to be done by hand.

An interesting production during the early part of the 20th century was the enormous quantity of china made for the splendid 'unsinkable Titanic'. This china was used by the 'flower of Europe's rich', sailing to America on the liner's maiden voyage. The dramatic pictures released of the undersea jetsam from the Titanic show great quantities of plates strewn over the sea bed. They have survived; the passengers did not.

The pattern produced for the Titanic is attractively simple.[15] A single plate is on loan to the Royal Crown Derby museum. An example is shown in the illustration, taken from the pre-launch leaflet.

Many 'Antiques Fairs' seem to produce some Parian-ware.[16] The lovely satiny sheen is peculiarly suited to the modelling of classical figures, often copied from antique statuary. The Victorians loved to decorate not only their homes and gardens, but also public parks, with 'Apollos' and 'Hebes'. Parian versions of these figures appeared in halls and drawing rooms and remained fashionable for many years.

Parian brooches, vases, baskets and flowers were also popular. The body was cheap to produce in spite of the many firing hours needed. Being highly vitrified it allowed crisp modelling, with the level of iron silicate affecting the colour —

"Titanic" sails on first voyage from Southampton to New York on Wednesday, April 10th, 1912.

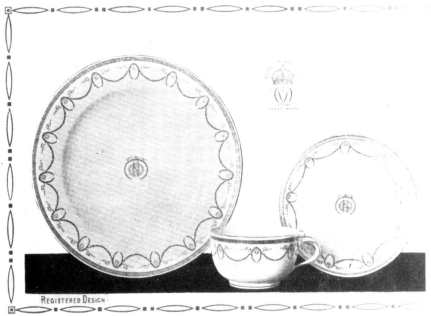

Illustrations[15]

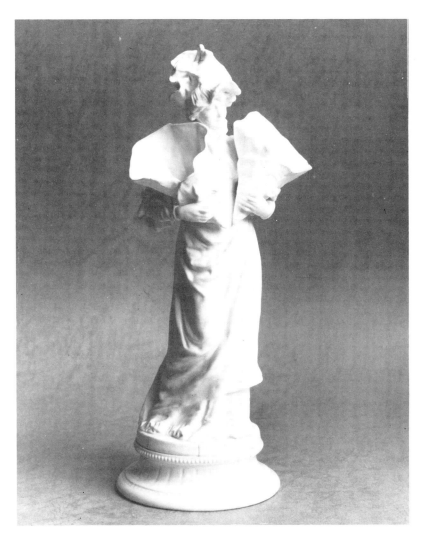

Illustration [16]

near white through to deep cream. The sculptor's skill demanded matching skill from the maker of the moulds, as is still the case today. An alabaster model would be cut into pieces so as to form the basis of the separate mould sections of the finished shape. As many as fifty separate sections might be involved. Shrinkage of up to one-quarter of the original size occurred in firing.

Very little Parianware was made at Derby and virtually the only surviving use of this lovely material is at Beleek, in Ireland. However, so popular was Parian that factories were established which produced nothing else.

Other interesting, useless but fun objects, introduced at Osmaston Road in 1904 but also made at both Nottingham Road and King Street, were miniatures. These lovely little pieces were tiny copies of tableware shapes although flat irons on stands, cauldrons, coal scuttles, hot water jugs and bowls were also made. These are often described as salesmen's samples, or as doll's house furnishings, but were really only intended for display. However, the larger miniatures may well have been for small girls to imitate their mothers' role as hostesses. The increasingly elaborate ritual of afternoon tea with Mama presiding over the teapot must have made these miniatures irresistible to little girls.

Production of miniatures continued until 1940. Having survived the artificially cocooned world of the wealthy during the First World War, china toys could not survive in a world of tin mugs in air raid shelters.

Miniatures are produced today, but in two patterns only — 'Posies' and 'Old Imari'. These are part of the world of collectables as are those old, and until recently undervalued survivors from an earlier age. For interest in miniatures we must again thank 'Antiques Road Show', without which the world of the collector would be a desert indeed.

The 1914-18 war, with its tragic and disastrous death toll of Europe's young men, introduced to the Derby factories (both Osmaston Road and King Street) the first really important influx of women painters and gilders. Previously women's work had been either hard or dirty, or dismissed as 'slight', meaning 'cheap' when applied to decoration. Women replaced the men who had left, many of whom would never return. The names of some of them are recorded in a small notebook in the Museum archives as 'gone to the War', with reference to the war itself as 'the greatest war in history'. Certainly the loss was great, in talent, in manpower and in children for women who now would never marry. Many women, like Mabel Winterson (aunt of Myra Challand), worked their entire lives in the Decorating Shop painting and gilding Imaris: poor pay, long days, weeks out of work when trade was slack, yet producing the wonderful work we now collect as antique *Derby*. The women who worked with Mabel Winterson are known only as faces in old photographs taken outside the factory.[17]

At King Street, during Derby's first Zeppelin raid in 1916 the kiln loading on that night was specially marked to commemorate what must have been a singular experience. The use of the crescent moon and Zeppelin on the back of the objects fired must have particular significance for those who can remember the occasion. Fortunately no bombs were dropped at the King Street end of the town.

The end of the war in 1918 brought an uneasy peace: shortages of food, houses and coal, strikes and more strikes. In Britain alone there were over 500 firms producing tableware, all competing for the same customers.

Illustration[17] *circa 1929*

The 1920s were difficult years for the workers, with short time and poor pay the reward for beautiful, careful work. The fine *Derby* artists of the period included Albert Gregory, who carried on the work and style of Desiré Leroy; Cuthbert Gresley of the Gresley water colour painting family; Marple and Dean,[18] both remembered for blue delft-type work; Reuben Hague for his classical plaques and Robert Barratt, whose birds and flowers were painted with naturalistic flair. These well-known artists were backed up by a team of generally unknown painters and gilders who produced the main stream work of very high quality.

Illustration [18] *A typical plate painted by W. E. J. Dean.*

Only in recent years, during reconstruction work, have some neglected corners of the Osmaston Road building been investigated to reveal old pictures, records, prints and production pieces. Amongst these was the artwork, by Albert Gregory, for a pattern called 'Aves', featuring golden pheasants and birds of paradise. This enduring design was originally inspired by an embroidered panel being worked by Miss Francis, at that time employed in the Showroom. In gold and coloured threads, it was being prepared for the Royal School of Needlework in London. About the same time as the accidental discovery of the artwork (instantly recognised by the knowledgeable lady who found it), the original embroidery was located in the attic of a house in the Isle of Wight, occupied by a nephew of Miss Francis. It was thus possible to have on display, for three months, the borrowed embroidered panel, the original artwork and the current production pattern.

Some of the 1880s figures were revived and figure production increased in the 1920s. Osmaston Road managed to prepare and present a prestigious collection for the Toronto Exhibition in 1925, and in the same year created a new Imari (Pattern 9571) for the Exposition des Arts Decoratifs in Paris, an event usually recognised as the summit of the Art Deco period.

But disaster was hovering close, both for England and her workers. The 1926 General Strike saw virtually every industry and every worker lose ground. The Depression, lack of work, lack of orders and the uneasy years following the 1929 Wall Street crash in America had meant disaster for many industries. Both King Street and Osmaston Road suffered reverses and worked at reduced capacity. This situation finally brought about a merger between the two companies. The 'Little Chap' was finally acquired in 1935 by its giant competitor for £4,000. The purchase price covered equipment, work people, the right to patterns, moulds and the old mark, with its 18th century Royal Charter.

The old Duesbury mark was then used occasionally, which still causes enormous identification problems for collectors. It is possible for figures marked in this way to be genuinely mistaken for King Street work of an earlier era.

Management during the period from 1929, at Osmaston Road, had been in the hands of Mr H. T. Robinson, who continued as Chairman of the merged companies until 1953.

There was an increased interest in the production of Imaris [19] during this time, carried out by women painters and gilders. Burnishing of the 22ct. gold was, as is the case today also performed by women, originally by rubbing the fired gold with agate and bloodstone to remove the sediment left on the surface after the final firing. This method has been replaced by the use of silver sand as the polishing medium, although there has been no substitute for patience.

1936 saw the launch of the film of H. G. Wells' book 'Things to come', and come they certainly did. The death of King George V, the accession and subsequent abdication of Edward VIII and the Coronation of King George VI all served to dampen public awarenesss of what was happening in Europe at that time, but by the summer of 1939 even the most unwilling realised that all was not well across the Channel and that 'something wicked this way comes'.

German troops invaded Poland in August 1939 and on Sunday 3rd September a tense nation heard Mr. Chamberlain announce that Britain was at war with Germany.

Wartime shortage of staff and materials made it difficult to keep up the level of production, with the majority of completed pieces of china being made for utilitarian purposes. There is, however, a surprisingly large number of very decorative *Derby* objects dating from the early years of the war. These elaborately decorated pieces of ware were sent to America as part of the Lease-Lend Agreement, and in effect helped to pay not only for arms, but for Spam and dried egg. By order of the Board of Trade this decorative production was later banned and only 'Utility', plain white glazed ware, was permitted.

After America entered the war in December 1941, tours of the factory were organised for American forces and their nursing personnel in Britain, in order to promote, hopefully, later peacetime contacts.

The period from 1945, exacerbated by the ending of American Aid, was as difficult for Britain as the war years had

Illustration [19]

been. Even more damaging than personal shortages, was the lack of essential raw materials. Furthermore, ways of encouraging ex-servicemen to return and young people to enter the industry had to be found. Despite a demonstrated willingness to rebuild post-war Britain, there was less enthusiasm for working in conditions more reminiscent of the Industrial Revolution than the 1950s 'brave new world'.

Improvements included ripping out parts of the old 1830s workhouse buildings, electricity replaced coal-fired bottle kilns and attempts to alleviate industrial hazards were made, to satisfy new health regulations. The marriage of Princess Elizabeth and Prince Philip in 1947 was an opportunity to demonstrate the return to peacetime production, when an old Regency pattern, 'Purple Scroll', was updated under a new name, 'Princess Scroll',[20] for presentation as a wedding gift.

A change of management, in 1953, saw Philip Robinson, son of the previous chairman, appointed to a post which eventually combined the work of art director, managing director and chairman. Philip Robinson at sometime had held the post of Professor of Free Fine Arts at Worcester College of Art. His 'P.R' figures have not survived as production models today, although some of his tableware patterns are still in use.

Illustration[20]

A range of field birds modelled by a Latvian refugee, Arnold Mikwlson, belongs to the same period. The barn owl is one of the birds from this collection. The original wooden sculptures were used as the basis for the moulds from which the figures are still made today.

In the same year the 'Queen's Vase', a composite production by Derby, Minton, Royal Doulton, Wedgwood, Spode and Worcester, was made for presentation to the Commonwealth Heads of State. Four years later, in 1957, 'Royal Pinxton Roses' was the Queen's choice for her personal use. The service was a gift to Her Majesty from the town.[21]

The wealth of the oil-rich Sheikhs of Kuwait and Saudi Arabia came to Derby in the 1950s to 1960s with orders for huge tableware services of 200 to 300 pieces. Certain shapes, such as dishes to contain a whole cooked sheep, were specially moulded. Plates lavish with cobalt, maroon and relief gilding might each have entailed eight hours' work on gilding alone.

Although at that time 85% of all *Derby* production was being exported, the factory was so badly in need of expensive renovation that only a takeover by Allied English Potteries saved the company from financial disaster. In 1969 a further change in management occurred when the company became a part of the Royal Doulton group, itself a subsidiary of the Pearson financial organisation. In the interests of economy many earlier patterns were withdrawn and warehouse stocks reduced to only the best selling lines. These measures, combined with efficient management by Mr Arthur Rigby, served to keep the factory functioning effectively. The fresh influx of money from the parent company allowed the old showroom under the dome — a Derby City landmark — to be transformed and opened as a museum by the Duchess of Devonshire, making it possible to see the factory's history from the 1740s on its home ground for the first time.

In 1972, a new range of patterns was introduced on an old shape called 'Queen's Gadroon'. The rich patterns, designed by June and Brian Branscombe, were launched using Kedleston Hall as a back drop. Unfortunately the Gadroon shape, in spite of its beauty and pedigree, did not appeal to

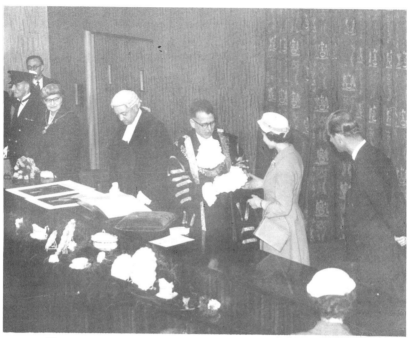

the customer, and was withdrawn from the range in the 1980s.

In spite of the recession which made trading difficult, and forced reduction in the workforce, production during the 1970s gradually expanded with some newly created designs. A connoisseur's collection of coffee cans in Scarsdale Yellow featuring water birds, painted by John McCloughlin, and a series of Derbyshire landscape plates by Michael Crawley [22] were introduced. These young painters, with Stefan Nowacki, trained under Albert Haddock, one of the finest of the 20th century gilders and painters. Haddock's long and varied career ended in 1983, although he continued to paint in his retirement.

After the retirement of Mr Rigby in 1986 the management of the company was taken over by Managing Director the Hon. Hugh Gibson and Chief Executive Mr John Bate, who have continued to carry the business on to success.

Illustration [22]

The 1980s was a time of continued improvement to outdated kilns and machinery. The old-fashioned reception area was restructured to present a more modern image and the 1830s workhouse building fronting Osmaston Road was reskinned with a layer of hand made bricks. The ornate gold crown, lost earlier from the dome in a storm, was replaced with a new version of the original in 1988.

There was a gradual return to economic stability in industry. At the Derby factory this meant increased work, a larger work force once again, and interesting additions to the product range. New thinking brought into prominence creatively different giftware. The paperweight range, modelled by Robert Jefferson, made a tremendous impact on the buying public. Moulding was simple and stylised, decoration traditional red, blue and gold.

The earliest paperweights, after their cautious launch, heralded many more interesting shapes, often for specific markets, such as the Far Eastern year symbols as in the Year of the Dragon.[23] The Australian bi centenary was marked by a platypus and koala; the R.S.P.B. centenary by a robin and chaffinch. Others followed to become readily available fun collectables.

New patterns for tableware were created to augment the long-lived, much-loved traditionals, and will hopefully themselves become part of those traditions.

Illustration [23]

A visit by then Prime Minister, Margaret Thatcher, in 1987 saw these new creations given unexpected prominence, when she insisted the photographers filmed her holding new work. An avid collector herself, she has proved to be an ambassador for the factory on many occasions.

Another visitor in 1988 was the Princess of Wales, whose official function was to open a splendid new extension to the factory museum. She carried on the tradition of past royal visits in great style, giving pleasure to the invited schoolchildren and workers during the course of a crowded day in Derby.

The new extension was created to house a wonderful collection of Victorian and Edwardian china, given to the Museum on permanent loan by a London cancer specialist, Mr Ronald Raven. The china is displayed in a Victorian room setting, on furniture from earlier periods also given by Mr Raven.

The extension houses a King Street section which allows greater prominence to be given to work from the period 1848 to 1935.

Thus an efficient and forward looking industry is allied to a comprehensive display of past excellence. Hopefully this allows the future to be built on to a solid foundation from the past.

Since William Duesbury first successfully established his factory on Nottingham Road the world has seen enormous changes — wars and revolts on the one hand, progress, both social and technological, on the other, all of which have changed our lives dramatically.

People are no longer so sharply divided into very rich or very poor. There are few homes with armies of servants, and few in England so poor that death in rags from starvation is inevitable. More of us are able to enjoy some level of luxury, owning pleasing objects from the past alongside treasures from the present. It is significant that the Derby factory can contribute both. Such continuing tradition of beauty and excellence deserves the pride of the city, county, country and people. Long may it continue to thrive.

AN A to Z of CERAMICS

BALL CLAY — A very plastic clay mined in Devon and Dorset. So named because it was originally mined as lumps or balls weighing about 14 Kg.

BISCUIT WARE — Also called bisque ware. It is pottery that has been fired but not glazed.

BLUNGER — A large vat in which raw materials in both liquid and solid form are mixed together.

BONE CHINA — The English form of porcelain. It is white, translucent and very strong. The key ingredient is bone ash.

CHINA — In Britain, this usually refers to bone china but is sometimes used to mean all forms of porcelain. So named because the Chinese were the first to make it.

CHINA CLAY — Derived from feldspar, it is the purest form of natural clay. It has a fine texture and, when fired, burns very white. In England it is mined in Cornwall.

CHINA STONE — Also called Cornish Stone. It is feldspar less decomposed than china clay and is used as a flux.

CLAY — The essential raw material for ceramics. It is found in many forms practically everywhere in the world. It is formed when rock breaks down under the action of the weather or by chemical processes — as in the case of china clay.

EARTHENWARE — Pottery fired at a relatively low temperature. This means that, unlike china, it is not vitrified but is porous, opaque and not so strong. It must be glazed if it is to hold liquids.

ENAMELLING — Enamel colours are metallic oxides ground to a fine powder with a flux added. Fired at a low temperature, it is used to decorate pottery that has already been glazed.

ENAMEL FIRING — A low temperature firing given to ware decorated on-glaze.

FAIENCE — A French term for any porous pottery body.

FELDSPAR — An ingredient of clays.

FILTER PRESS — A press used to extract water from slip.

FIRING — Baking ware in a kiln.

FLATWARE — Ware such as plates and saucers.

FLINT — Ground flint is mixed with some pottery bodies to control expansion in the kiln.

GILDING — Using gold or platinum to decorate china.

GLAZES — A thin coating of liquid glass applied to most ware.

GLOST-FIRING — The firing given to ware after glazing.

HOLLOWARE — Ware such as cups, teapots and vegetable dishes.

JIGGERING — Shaping flatware such as plates with a machine called a jigger. A pancake of clay is sandwiched between a revolving plaster mould (which forms the front of the plate) and a metal profile-tool (which forms the back).

JOLLEYING — The same principle as jiggering applied to cups — the mould forms the outside and the profile-tool the inside.

KAOLIN — Another name for china clay.

KILNS — Heated chambers used for baking ware. They vary greatly in size, in the way they operate and the fuel they use. The two main types are 'intermittent' and 'tunnel' kilns.

LITHOGRAPHS — Transfers used to decorate ware.

MOULDS — Normally made of plaster of paris and used extensively for shaping both plastic and liquid clay.

ON-GLAZE — Decoration of ware after the glaze has been fired.

PORCELAIN — The general term for a vitrified, white and translucent material. In Britain, it normally refers to ware made from a feldspathic body and is thus distinguished from bone china.

PUG MILL — Rather like a giant mincing machine. It kneads the clay to remove all bubbles of air and give it an even consistency.

REFRACTORIES — Materials which can withstand very high temperatures. Fireclay is an example.

SLIP — Clay and water mixed to a creamy consistency. Slip is made as a means of accurately mixing the ingredients of a pottery body (in which case it is then filter-pressed) or to be used for casting ware in plaster moulds.

SLIP-CASTING — Casting with liquid clay.

STONEWARE — A vitreous but opaque pottery body.

THROWING — A method of shaping holloware. A ball of clay is thrown onto a revolving potter's wheel, is centred and then shaped by the hands.

UNDER-GLAZE — Decoration of ware before glazing.

VITRIFICATION — When clay is fired one of the constituents — silica — is changed into glass and bonds all the other ingredients together. As vitrification proceeds the proportion of glassy bond increases and its porosity becomes lower. China is fully vitrified.

NOTTINGHAM ROAD FACTORY 1748 to 1848

EARLY DERBY INDICATED BY 'DRY-EDGE' — GLAZE WHICH STOPS SHORT OF
THE EDGE OF THE FIGURE'S BASE

PATCH MARKS — THREE DARKER PATCHES ON BASE WHERE FIGURE STOOD
ON BALLS OF CLAY DURING FIRING

 RICHARD HOLDSHIP 1764 to 1769

    ORIENTAL TYPE MARKS 1765 to 1780

 INCISED MARKS ON DISHES 1770 to 1780

  CHELSEA — DERBY (IN GOLD) 1769 to 1775

 DERBY AFTER ROYAL WARRANT GRANTED BY
GEORGE III 1775 to 1782

 INCISED UNDER FIGURES   HAND-PAINTED MARKS
PUCE, BLUE OR BLACK 1782-1800 neatly
RED 1800-1825 carelessly

 DUESBURY AND KEAN — 1795 — RARE

  LATE DUESBURY MARKS — VERY RARE

BLOOR

 1811

 1820 to 1840 PRINTED

 PRINTED IN RED 1825 to 1840

 MOCK MEISSEN 1785 to 1825

 MOCK SÈVRES 1825 to 1848

 RED PRINTED 1830 to 1848

KING STREET FACTORY 1848 to 1935

 1849 to 1859

 1849 to 1863

 1859 to 1861

 1861 to 1935 —— Painted or printed old mark in red, blue or puce. 'S & H' at first used to indicate partnership of Stephenson and Hancock, later sole proprietor Sampson Hancock.

 WILLIAM LARCOMBE 1916

 LARCOMBE AND PAGET 1917-1934

 PAGET AND PAGET 1934

} Used in conjunctio
with the old mark

OSMASTON ROAD FACTORY 1877 to 1890
DERBY PORCELAIN CO. LTD.

1878 to 1890 PLUS YEAR CYPHERS
CROWN EARTHENWARE

IMPRESSED INTO CLAY (DATES MAY
ALSO OCCUR i.e. 3.99 (MARCH 1899))
'DERBY' IMPRESSED INTO CLAY
ON CHINA 1878 to 1900 (SOMETIMES
LATER)

ROYAL CROWN DERBY PORCELAIN CO. LTD.
ROYAL WARRANT GRANTED 1st JULY 1890

1890 PLUS YEAR CYPHERS
'MADE IN ENGLAND' REPLACED 'ENGLAND' IN 1921

WARTIME MARK 1940 to 1955
ALSO USED ON WHITE UTILITY WARE

1964 to 1975 PLUS YEAR CYPHERS

1976 TO PRESENT DAY PLUS CYPHERS

YEAR CYPHERS

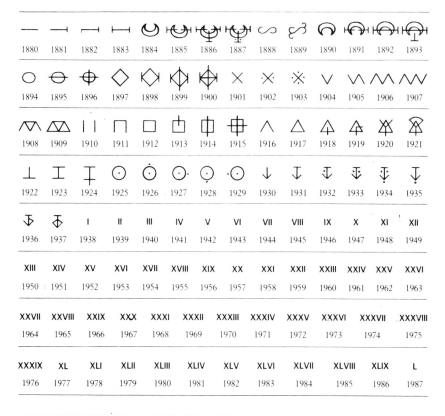

| 1880 | 1881 | 1882 | 1883 | 1884 | 1885 | 1886 | 1887 | 1888 | 1889 | 1890 | 1891 | 1892 | 1893 |

| 1894 | 1895 | 1896 | 1897 | 1898 | 1899 | 1900 | 1901 | 1902 | 1903 | 1904 | 1905 | 1906 | 1907 |

| 1908 | 1909 | 1910 | 1911 | 1912 | 1913 | 1914 | 1915 | 1916 | 1917 | 1918 | 1919 | 1920 | 1921 |

| 1922 | 1923 | 1924 | 1925 | 1926 | 1927 | 1928 | 1929 | 1930 | 1931 | 1932 | 1933 | 1934 | 1935 |

| I | II | III | IV | V | VI | VII | VIII | IX | X | XI | XII |
| 1936 | 1937 | 1938 | 1939 | 1940 | 1941 | 1942 | 1943 | 1944 | 1945 | 1946 | 1947 | 1948 | 1949 |

| XIII | XIV | XV | XVI | XVII | XVIII | XIX | XX | XXI | XXII | XXIII | XXIV | XXV | XXVI |
| 1950 | 1951 | 1952 | 1953 | 1954 | 1955 | 1956 | 1957 | 1958 | 1959 | 1960 | 1961 | 1962 | 1963 |

| XXVII | XXVIII | XXIX | XXX | XXXI | XXXII | XXXIII | XXXIV | XXXV | XXXVI | XXXVII | XXXVIII |
| 1964 | 1965 | 1966 | 1967 | 1968 | 1969 | 1970 | 1971 | 1972 | 1973 | 1974 | 1975 |

| XXXIX | XL | XLI | XLII | XLIII | XLIV | XLV | XLVI | XLVII | XLVIII | XLIX | L |
| 1976 | 1977 | 1978 | 1979 | 1980 | 1981 | 1982 | 1983 | 1984 | 1985 | 1986 | 1987 |

BECAUSE BOTH 1904 and 1942 USE A 'V' SYMBOL THE FIRST IS ACCOMPANIED BY 'ENGLAND' AND LATER BY 'MADE IN ENGLAND'

THE YEAR 1901 and 1947 USE 'X' AND THE SAME DIFFERENTIATION IS USED

NAMES OF COMMISSIONING COMPANIES OR STOCKISTS MAY SOMETIMES BE FOUND ACCOMPANYING THE FACTORY MARK, AS MAY THE NAME OF THE PATTERN.

PATTERN NUMBERS WHERE THEY OCCUR ON EARLY PIECES ARE NORMALLY HAND-PAINTED, BUT PRINTED ON LATER WORK.

ACKNOWLEDGMENTS

I would like to acknowledge with gratitude the help I have received from my colleagues at Royal Crown Derby and Royal Doulton, for access to archival material and photography; to Derby Local Study Library; to Derby Museum and Art Gallery for permission to use the photograph of the Prentice Plate; the Industrial Museum for the photograph of the present factory; to my husband for his patience and to my son for his encouragement.

The following books and material have been essential for my study and those interested in pursuing the subject further will find them useful and illuminating. The list is not intended as a comprehensive bibliography.

Chelsea China	*Llewellyn Jewitt*
Derby, an Illustrated History	*Maxwell Craven*
Derby, Bow and Chelsea China	*William Bemrose*
Derby China	*Llewellyn Jewitt*
Derby Porcelain	*John Twitchett*
Eighteenth Century Porcelain Figures	*Peter Bradshaw*
Japanese Porcelain	*Hazel Gorham*
Royal Crown Derby	*John Twitchett and Betty Bailey*
T'ang Pottery and Porcelain	*Margaret Medley*
The Old Derby China Manufactory	*John Haslem*
The Potteries	*David Sekers*

THE DERBYSHIRE HERITAGE SERIES

Titles in the series:

Other published titles: